IMPROVING YOUR COMPANY IMAGE

A Do-It-Yourself Guide

Sylvia Ann Blishak

CRISP PUBLICATIONS, INC.
Los Altos, California

IMPROVING YOUR COMPANY IMAGE
A Do-It-Yourself Guide

Sylvia Ann Blishak

CREDITS:
Editor: **Kay Kepler**
Designer: **Carol Harris**
Typesetting: **ExecuStaff**
Cover Design: **Carol Harris**
Artwork: **Ralph Mapson**

Copyright © 1992 Crisp Publications, Inc.
Printed in the United States of America by Bawden Printing Company.

English language Crisp books are distributed worldwide. Our major international distributors include:

CANADA: Reid Publishing, Ltd., Box 69559—109 Thomas St., Oakville, Ontario Canada L6J 7R4. TEL: (416) 842-4428, FAX: (416) 842-9327

AUSTRALIA: Career Builders, P.O. Box 1051, Springwood, Brisbane, Queensland, Australia 4127. TEL: 841-1061, FAX: 841-1580

NEW ZEALAND: Career Builders, P.O. Box 571, Manurewa, Auckland, New Zealand. TEL: 266-5276, FAX: 266-4152

JAPAN: Phoenix Associates Co., Mizuho Bldg. 2-12-2, Kami Osaki, Shinagawa-Ku, Tokyo 141, Japan. TEL: 3-443-7231, FAX: 3-443-7640

Selected Crisp titles are also available in other languages. Contact International Rights Manager Tim Polk at (415) 949-4888 for more information.

Library of Congress Catalog Card Number 91-76245
Blishak, Sylvia Ann
Improving Your Company Image
ISBN 1-56052-136-8

This book is printed on recyclable paper with soy ink.

PRINTED WITH SOY INK

ABOUT THIS BOOK

This book will appeal to you if you are:

Thinking about starting an enterprise.

Outgrowing, along with your organization, an image that was appropriate a few years ago.

Managing a small association that has grown, a larger one that has downsized or one that has been through a merger or a change of ownership.

Contemplating a change of location, an expansion, a new product line or service, a branch—or any step that will change the nature of your organization.

Wondering if your established enterprise is in a rut and could profit by an updated or more focused identity.

At loose ends because your staff is confused about what the goals of the organization are.

Colorful examples will illustrate how the first impressions that organizations project can work for (or against) their success. You will get involved in understanding and analyzing your own entity's culture—with questions that only you can answer.

By the time you're finished, you will have a clearer picture of how your organization's image comes across to your customers and what you can do to enhance it.

Good luck!

Sylvia Ann Blishak

Sylvia Ann Blishak

CONTENTS

CONTENTS (continued)

SHOULD YOU READ THIS BOOK?

Yes—if your organization interfaces with other people.

The focus of *Improving Your Company's Image* is on finding new ways to analyze and project an identity that is a true and conscious reflection of the personality and goals of the management.

This book isn't just for entrepreneurs, retailers and service businesses—you may apply the same guidelines if you're a part of a:

- Nonprofit association

- Government office

- Health organization

- Financial institution

- Utility company

- Sports team or musical group

- Any association that works with other people or organizations.

What can an enhanced image do for you if you're not selling anything or competing with anyone?

It can make your job easier and more pleasant! A neglected, poorly communicated or outdated image can confuse the people you interact with. And that can make your job difficult if people are:

► **Confused**—because they'll take up your time with unnecessary questions, or

► **Annoyed**—because you'll be resolving unnecessary complaints.

WHAT THIS BOOK IS AND ISN'T

This book is not a treatise on expensive cosmetic makeovers—although what your customers see is important and can make an indelible first impression.

But enhancing your organization's image isn't as simple as hiring someone to select a new color for your stationery or to suggest that you change the type of background music you play. What customers perceive must match the personality of your enterprise. Advertising, public relations and marketing are all important expressions of your image. But to make your investment in these expensive endeavors pay off, you'll need to have a clear understanding of your organization's identity.

This Book *Will* Explore Do-It-Yourself Ways To:	This Book *Won't* Insist You Spend Thousands of ''Quick-Fix'' Dollars To:
• Make you more aware of the impression your entity is projecting • Discover whether your present image is consistent with your entity's goals and appeals to the customers you want • Update your organization's image as its status changes: from startup to established, from general to specialty, from small to large	• Hire a corporate culture consultant to invent a new name • Have a decorator redo your office in this year's color scheme or outfit your staff with matching uniforms • Commission an expensive custom-designed logo and have all your stationery, business cards and signs redone

After you've learned more about how an image works, you may decide to call in professional help.

S E C T I O N

I

The Nuts and Bolts of an Image

HOW AN IMAGE WORKS FOR—OR AGAINST—AN ORGANIZATION

Sometimes one small, jarring note can be so inappropriate that it can destroy a carefully conceived, tasteful and expensively produced image.

Example

An upscale grocery store, already noted for its attractive decor and excellent customer service, just spent several million dollars on expansion and redesign. The market ran expensive four-page ads in the paper to promote its lavish grand opening with guest celebrities and free food and drink. The store now contains a coffee bar, a wine-tasting room and a cooking school.

But the high-class image suffers when employees loiter on the sidewalk outside the front entrance at break time, smoking cigarettes and leaning or sitting on the shopping carts.

GETTING TO KNOW YOUR OWN ORGANIZATION'S IMAGE

Does your enterprise's first impression give your customers a good idea of what to expect? Is the identity it portrays a successful one that will encourage people to do business with you?

If you're like many busy managers and entrepreneurs, you're probably so busy running your organization that you haven't had much time to think about such questions. And you may draw a blank when you try to answer them.

We're going to help you to be more aware of the impression your enterprise makes. Then you can decide what practical steps you want to take to make it work more effectively for you.

Images: Everything Counts

You walk into an unfamiliar restaurant. The waitress who greets you is wearing crepe-soled shoes and a stained uniform. "Be with you in a minute, Honey!" she says as she tucks a pencil behind her ear.

You've just been zapped by an image—that important impression that grabs you within the first seconds of starting a transaction. Instantly, just from encountering one employee, you've learned a lot about what to expect from this restaurant.

You would probably expect to find filling ''comfort food'' like French fries with gravy or chicken-fried steak on the menu. And you wouldn't be surprised if the nonsmoking section were small or nonexistent.

You've only been exposed to a small part of this restaurant's identity. Yet already you've been strongly influenced.

Is the waitress portraying an outdated image? Is the management consciously appealing to customers who enjoy traditional, hearty food? Or does management think about image at all?

These are the kinds of questions you'll be asking yourself about your organization. And, since the business climate, your clients' tastes and needs and your own situation change constantly, we'll talk about how to schedule periodic reality checkups for your organization's image.

WHAT IS IMAGE?

AN IMAGE CONSISTS OF INGREDIENTS COMBINED IN A UNIQUE WAY

Notice what pictures come to mind as you visualize some possible ''identity ingredients.'' Imagine:

1. **Staff members**—wearing shorts, speaking in a monotone or chewing gum

2. **Background noise**—clanging machinery, ringing telephones or employees yelling at each other across the office

3. **Background music**—hard rock, country and western, rap, insipid elevator music or classical

4. **Color**—rosewood furniture, orange shag carpets or stained glass windows

5. **Arrangement**—a display with one or two pieces of luggage artfully arranged, a window with a jumble of purses, shoes and belts with price tags attached or a rack of dusty, faded brochures

6. **Smell**—permanent waves and peroxide as you step into a beauty shop, fine perfume in a department store or stale cooking oil in a restaurant.

7. Add your own: _____

_____

_____

We've just scratched the surface of the many facets of an organization's image. Now, it's your turn. What sensory factors have grabbed you lately when you:

Walked into a store or office?

_____

_____

_____

Telephoned?

_____

_____

_____

Glanced at a direct mail ad?

_____

_____

_____

Saw a magazine or newspaper ad for the first time?

_____

_____

_____

Saw a TV ad for the first time?

_____

_____

_____

EVERY ORGANIZATION HAS AN IMAGE

You've never hired a package designer or a public relations firm or an advertising agency—does that mean you don't have an image?

Every organization projects its own unique image. You may not have given your own much thought. Or you may have paid a great deal for a graphic designer to create stationery and business cards and brochures to your specifications. Perhaps you've hired an interior decorator to coordinate your furniture and equipment with attractive artwork and pleasant colors. Or it may be a sort of aura that you and your staff are not really aware of—yet an image is an energy source as constant as the force of gravity.

Even the Garbage Company Has an Image

Browning Ferris Industries (BFI) collects garbage in Canada, the United States of America and in Europe, providing a service that will never be out of date or unnecessary. Does this giant international corporation worry about its image?

Yes—even the garbage company publishes an annual report for stockholders and prospective investors. BFI spent a handsome sum to send a San Francisco photographer and his assistant to Spain and the Netherlands to photograph some of its employees.

WHY CUSTOMERS RETURN

Recall some establishments with which you trade frequently. Describe their atmosphere. Pretend you are talking to someone who knows nothing about these enterprises, but is considering doing business with them and wonders what they're really like.

Your bank _____

_____

_____

Your favorite restaurant _____

_____

_____

Your favorite movie theater _____

_____

_____

Your barber or beauty shop _____

_____

_____

Your grocery store _____

_____

_____

Do you feel that the ambience these establishments portray is an accidental evolution? Or has it been carefully thought out? Is the aura consistent, or are there pieces that don't seem to fit?

Now reread your descriptions, and jot down your answers.

HOW A POOR IMAGE CAN ALIENATE YOUR CUSTOMERS

If it's neglected, decor can portray a careless, ignorant or out-of-date identity.

Too Busy to Be Up-to-Date

A travel agency decorates its glass doors with colorful airline decals.

"This will catch people's eyes and demonstrate that we offer many options to the air traveler," reasoned the owner. *But that was three years ago.* Now, due to mergers and bankruptcies, many of the air carriers that provided the decals are out of business.

What would you think if you wanted to buy an airline ticket and walked into the agency with defunct airlines' decals as part of the decor?

_____

Would you expect this agency to have up-to-date fare and schedule information?

_____

Would you expect the staff to be aware of the latest developments in the airline industry?

_____

Is this such a successful, busy enterprise that nobody has had time to update the window display?

_____

Is this an agency that is not only careless about their decor but careless about their approach to trip planning, too?

_____

Would you feel confident about booking your trip with this agency?

_____

The Advertised Image that Doesn't Match Expectations

A new hotel sent an expensive brochure and cover letter to executive secretaries. The mailing promoted an elegant, upscale property offering the finest personalized service. But when one secretary called the hotel with a question, here's what happened:

1. She was put on hold by a receptionist.

2. Instead of music she listened to a recorded hard-sell message for the hotel.

3. Then a reservationist came on and said, ''Sorry this is taking so long, Shirley, but I can't find your booking in the computer. Have you mailed us a deposit yet?'' (The secretary explained that she wasn't Shirley and hadn't made a booking.)

4. She was put on hold a second time.

5. A third voice came on the line and answered her question. When the secretary thanked her, the voice said, ''That's OK, Sugar,'' and hung up.

6. The executive secretary threw the brochure away in irritation, aware that the fancy mailing piece did not match the type of service the hotel offered. ''My boss would be furious if I booked him into a place like that,'' she said to herself.

> Any organization's image makes an instant imprint on the eyes, ears and emotions of the prospect. It will override expectations created by advertising, sales techniques and marketing approaches.

HOW IMAGE ADVERTISING DIFFERS FROM PRODUCT-ADVANTAGE ADVERTISING

Some organizations make a conscious effort to alter the way they're perceived in the public eye by extensive ''image advertising''—which links their product to a certain lifestyle or cause, rather than listing the benefits involved in using it.

The Pepsi Generation ads are an example of lifestyle image advertising. So are most perfume ads, which tell you little about the fragrance of the product but a lot about the glamour and mystery your persona will acquire—and the adventures you may have as a result—should you wear the product. Stuart Ewen's book, *All Consuming Images,** mentions ''. . . commercials . . . telling us of the . . . way that Henry Grethel clothing will lead us into accidental and anonymous romantic encounters with beautiful women—or men—in elegant hotel rooms.''

In the 1960s and 1970s, oil companies claimed that if you put their products in your car, it would run better. Today, air and water pollution (for which the petroleum and automotive industries are largely responsible) are becoming important issues. Certain oil, automobile and power companies are attempting to align themselves with environmental causes by running advertisements with photos of scenic wilderness areas or wildlife refuges. These companies have shifted to image advertising.

---

*Harper Collins Publishers (Basic Books)

A strong image communicates a clear message about the personality of your enterprise and why your product or service is special.

Write a few words describing your organization:

_____

_____

_____

_____

_____

_____

This is what our enterprise does: _____

_____

_____

_____

We are in this field because: _____

_____

_____

_____

Our product or service is unique because: _____

_____

_____

_____

S E C T I O N

II

Examples of Images

OTHER ORGANIZATIONS' IMAGES

EXAMPLE 1	*An inexpensive and appealing professional image makes advertising unnecessary*

Going to an electrologist (where unwanted hair is removed with an electric needle) can be an anxiety-producing experience, but Gerry Hunter, C.P.E., of Menlo Park, California, has created such a comfortably reassuring identity for her practice that clients often come early.

Her office is decorated with original landscape paintings. "One of my patients is an artist, and I let her display her work here," she admits. Hunter keeps several puzzles and a bowl of hard candy on a table next to the sofa in the waiting room. Soft classical music, numerous current magazines, and informative literature about the electrological procedure add to the ambiance.

Hunter designed her office's image not by hiring an expensive interior decorator but by putting herself in a prospective patient's shoes. " 'Does it hurt? Is it really permanent? How do I know the electrologist knows what she's doing?' All these questions run through a person's mind," says Hunter.

She also makes it a point to acknowledge patients as soon as they come in. Even if she's busy, she greets them enthusiastically and says "I'll be with you soon!"

Image result: Even during the recent recession, Hunter's practice was growing by two or three referrals every week. She had to hire an associate to help handle all her business.

OTHER ORGANIZATIONS' IMAGES
(continued)

EXAMPLE 2   *A sign of success*

A well-known, successful real estate agent has his own clearly defined and original image. "A messy desk is a sign of success," this agent is fond of saying. "If you have a neat, empty desk, your clients will think you have nothing to do."

Do you agree? While this image is consistent with his creative and innovative personality, it might not work for—or appeal to—everyone.

Imagine walking into his office and seeing his desk piled high with papers, contracts and reference books. What does that desk say to you about the expertise and efficiency of this agent?

_____

Now imagine walking into another real estate agency down the street. The staff in this office have all their reference material filed away, and their desks are neat and empty.

What do these desks convey to you about the expertise and efficiency of this enterprise?

_____

Which real estate agency do you suppose would handle the sale of your property in the way you'd be most comfortable with?

_____

How does your desk look? _____

Is your desk management in accord with your own personality and the goals of your enterprise?

_____

_____

Are you comfortable with your "desk image" or would you like to change it?

_____

EXAMPLE 3   *Using existing resources in a new way*

A bakery in a shopping mall set up an exhaust fan outlet over the sidewalk so pedestrians would be tempted by the irresistible aroma of fresh-baked goodies.

Savvy identity crafters keep looking for innovative and positive ways to make their image energy work for them.

Before you scrutinize your own organization's identity, it will help to learn more about how other organizational cultures work or don't work. So start looking at businesses and stores around your own community in a new light. What kind of image do they project? Enterprises within the same industry can create an amazing variety of personalities to present to the consumer, so choose one category (starting with a field other than your own while you're getting the hang of it) and compare those competing in it.

But before you start your legwork, we'll do an armchair exercise.

AN ARMCHAIR EXERCISE: TRAVEL AGENCIES

Case Study A

Continental Travel Planners is in an office building a block west of Main Street. The agency's name is lettered on the window in low-key gold characters. The decor is austere and bland. There are no posters to catch the eye. Clients must come in through the parking lot entrance into the building's lobby. The owner sits in a semi-enclosed office near the front where he can keep an eye on his quiet, businesslike staff.

Why does this agency keep such a low profile? Continental Travel Planners does not attract walk-in traffic—it actually discourages the casual browser.

Since it handles the business travel for an electronics company a few miles away, most of its bookings are transacted by telephone. Let's label this agency commerical.

Analysis:

Continental Travel Planners' image is almost completely consistent with its commercial travel focus. But the image doesn't match the name. That's because the character of the business has changed over the years. Continental was started as a small vacation agency by a specialist in continental tours.

She had trouble with the name, too. Although she wanted consistent, year-round business from domestic air tickets to supplement the seasonal European bookings, the agency's name confused many people who thought that she would book only European trips.

When the continental tour specialist sold Continental Travel Planners, the agency's new owner changed its image. He brought in the commercial account, tore down the European travel posters, expanded the staff and moved out of the retail district to larger quarters in a professional building. Even though "Continental Travel Planners" no longer describes the agency's specialty, the new owner kept the old name because he didn't want to confuse—and risk losing—the many clients who'd booked their European trips with the agency for years.

If you owned Continental Travel Planners, would you change its name?

_____

Can you think of a name that would convey the current personality of the agency without losing the identity that its European-bound customers are familiar with?

_____

_____

AN ARMCHAIR EXERCISE: TRAVEL AGENCIES (continued)

Case Study B

Jones Travel features expensive antique furniture, potted palms, Oriental rugs and state-of-the-art computer equipment. Classical music plays softly in the background. A bank of large wall clocks displaying time in different parts of the world faces the entry area; there are no brochures on display.

Customers are greeted at a reception counter and directed to the appropriate specialist. One agent is a cruise expert, another is a whiz at planning customized foreign itineraries, a third knows all about African safaris.

The agents at Jones Travel collect advance deposits before confirming reservations. And unlike most travel agencies, this one levies high service charges.

Since the staff members are experts at planning unusual itineraries to out-of-the-way places, customers willingly pay extra for these services. In fact, being a client of Jones Travel has a certain status in the community.

Analysis:

What kind of customer does Jones Travel's image appeal to?

_____

_____

How would you react if you came in as a casual shopper wanting to gather information on vacation options and the receptionist assigned you to one of the specialists who could only discuss cruises? Would you stay or leave?

_____

_____

_____

_____

What would you do if you wanted to plan an African safari, and the specialist in that department asked you for a $500 deposit before confirming your reservation?

_____

_____

_____

_____

Which word or phrase would you choose to label Jones Travel?

_____

_____

AN ARMCHAIR EXERCISE: TRAVEL AGENCIES (continued)

Case Study C

Two blocks from Jones Travel is Mainstreet Travel, located on the corner in a busy downtown area. The agency has big display windows. A cluttered collection of colorful travel displays and posters featuring a variety of destinations and models of ships and airplanes catches the sunlight. The front section of the office is devoted to brochure racks; agents sit at desks near the rear.

Analysis:

Do you think browsers are welcome here? _____

Would you guess that this is a new agency or one that's been here for several years?

_____

Does Mainstreet Travel have a speciality? _____

If you were planning on booking a complex, customized trip to India or South America would you feel confident about doing it through Mainstreet Travel?

_____

_____

If not, with which of the agencies described would you want to book your complex trip?

_____

What kind of customer will be drawn to Mainstreet Travel?

_____

Is there one word or phrase you would choose to describe Mainstreet Travel's image?

_____

Putting People in the Picture

A woman walks into Mainstreet Travel. She carries an African safari brochure under her arm. She's selected the tour she wants and the date of departure. She walks past the stands and racks of brochures and sits down next to one of the desks, gets out her checkbook, and waits for an agent to help her. One is on the phone and the other is having a lengthy consultation with a customer who is vacillating between a Club Med resort and a Caribbean cruise.

Meanwhile, a couple with two young children walk into Jones Travel down the street—the one with the receptionist and bank of clocks displaying time in various countries. They have an idea that they'd like to take their first cruise. But they need to know which ships might be appropriate for children and whether the food will appeal to kids. They'd like to collect some brochures but notice there aren't any on display.

Intimidated by the quiet, no-nonsense atmosphere, they leave and head toward Mainstreet Travel, remembering that they saw its big window displays as they drove downtown.

On the way, they pass a woman coming out with an African safari brochure and a determined look. Unable to get past the shoppers and information-gatherers to book her trip, she's on her way to faster and more businesslike service at the agency with the clocks. (The clocks indicate that Jones will book travel all over the world and hint that this agency, with its highly organized system, values staff and client time.)

Both customers have reacted to the images projected by these two agencies by realizing that they were in the wrong place. They are now headed in the right direction for their own particular needs.

FINDING THE NICHE THAT NOBODY ELSE HAS FILLED

Even though your enterprise may not be a travel agency, some of these ideas may inspire you to look at your own field of endeavor in a new light. If you were thinking of starting your own travel agency, you'd be looking for an identity that would make yours unique.

How could you build an original image in the community where the example agencies are located?

- You could specialize in sports and adventure travel

- You could open a ''cruise only'' agency

- You could specialize in rail travel

- You could be open during hours when the other agencies aren't; for example, you could use ''Your Saturday Travel Agency,'' or ''After Hours Travel Planning'' as slogans.

What other different kinds of image building blocks might you use to craft a special niche for your travel agency?

_____

_____

_____

_____

_____

_____

_____

_____

_____

_____

_____

_____

S E C T I O N

III

Names and Images

Made by the Complete Bathtub, Co.

WHAT'S IN A NAME?

> **A name is part of an image.**

As we've seen from some of the travel agency examples, businesses named for locations—such as a town or a street—aren't giving customers much of a clue about their uniqueness or their speciality. But they are defining place. If you run the only establishment of its type in your city and are competing with establishments in other towns, it may make sense to name your enterprise after the community.

But a location name is limiting should your organization move to another street or city—you'll have to decide whether to change the name of the organization and risk losing its identity.

Will your customers look in the phone book and, not finding your old name, call your competition? _____

Would it be better to keep the familiar location-identity name even though it no longer defines the location of the establishment? _____

One example of a limiting location-identity name was that of Eastern Airlines. During the 1970s, Eastern expanded out of the east coast of the United States and became a nationwide airline. But Eastern didn't survive as a cross-country carrier—it eventually cut back on its routes and went out of business. Perhaps its name, which gave it the identity of a regional airline, was part of the problem.

How might Eastern Airlines have modified or changed its name to match its expanded horizons without losing its identity?

_____

_____

_____

_____

_____

_____

_____

WHAT'S IN A NAME? (continued)

Messing with Success

Meanwhile, top dog United Airlines continued to prosper and grow with a name that was linked, in the mind of the traveling public, to ''United States.''

United's routes were expanding. Previously limited to flights within North America, United now became a world-wide airline, adding flights to Europe, Asia and the South Pacific.

Ignoring the time-worn truth that advises, ''If it ain't broke, don't fix it,'' a faction of United Airlines' management decided that their corporation, with its expanded focus, should have a trendy new name. The result was an appellation with no meaning—but with image potential—''Allegis.'' The airline began issuing ticket jackets with the unfamiliar, controversial Allegis name. And an expensive advertising campaign was launched to explain the change.

But cooler heads eventually prevailed, and the familiar United Airlines corporate identity was re-established.

Changing corporate names became quite a fad in the 1980s. And some of the new names didn't mean anything. Sometimes corporations simply adopted initials rather than words. Customers find initials easier to remember if they stand for a name they know such as International Business Machines (IBM). But do you know what TRW, SCM, SRI or FMC stand for?

_____

_____

_____

_____

_____

_____

If you must change your name, don't leave your customers behind. Make it similar enough so that people can still find you under the same alphabetical listing. (For example, Western International Hotels is now Westin Hotels.)

TIMELY NAMES

Consider the image of Twentieth Century Fox movie studios. Would you react to that image differently if it had been named ''Nineteenth Century Fox''?

In a few years, names that start with ''Twentieth Century'' will change from a timely image to an outdated one. Already, there are enterprises that call themselves ''Twenty-First Century Widgets.''

If you owned a company with ''Twentieth Century'' in its name, would you change it? _____

When would you make the change, and why? _____

_____

Names with a forward-looking and futuristic image can become inappropriate and outdated by changing circumstances and times. For example, in the 1950s, Alaska and Hawaii raced to achieve statehood. Many businesses in both Alaska and Hawaii reflected this enthusiasm by calling themselves ''Forty-Ninth State Bakery,'' or ''Forty-Ninth State Realty.''

When Alaska was admitted as the 49th U.S. state, the Alaskan entrepreneurs who'd used the name had images that sounded good and are still appropriate today. But the ''Forty-Ninth State'' businesses in Hawaii didn't maintain the same image when the island territory was admitted as the country's 50th state—yet several years after statehood, the Honolulu phone book still listed a few ''Forty-Ninth State'' businesses.

If you had owned a ''Forty-Ninth State'' business in Hawaii, would you have changed its name after statehood? _____

Why? _____

_____

How Changing Technology Can Make a Name Obsolete

Early in the century, there was a railroad called ''The Seaboard Airline.'' Since its route was ''as the crow flies,'' the name meant that their tracks, as seen from the *air* by that crow, would look like a straight *line*—thus air-line. This innovative moniker became very confusing when airline companies came into being. Eventually, after a merger, the railroad became ''The Seaboard Coast Line.''

RISKS IN CHANGING A NAME

People sometimes resist change. This is natural. Think of a company you know of that changed its name.

_____

Do you know why the name was changed?

_____

If you know why, do you agree with the reason?

_____

Do you ever forget the new name?

_____

Are you annoyed at having to remember the new name, or do you like it?

_____

Do you ever catch yourself referring to the company by its old name?

_____

Does the new name, in your opinion, more clearly define the enterprise and what it offers?

_____

Changing your company's name has advantages and pitfalls. You can reposition your image to attract new customers, but you may lose old ones in the process.

BUILDING A PERSONALITY INTO A NAME

Northwest Airlines, based in Minneapolis, began calling itself Northwest *Orient* Airlines when it began service to Asia. Now that the carrier has established a presence in the Orient, it has gone back to being Northwest Airlines again.

Super Glue has a name that describes the product.

Dreyer's *Grand* Ice Cream (known as Edy's Grand Ice Cream east of the Rocky Mountains) has created an appealing and successful image by adding ''Grand'' to its name. Yet the ''Grand'' is a reference to the original location of the company's first store on Grand Avenue in Oakland, California! Although the address has changed, the word ''Grand'' has been retained over the years as a reminder of the quality of Dreyer's ice cream.

The *Famous* Fourth Street Deli in Philadelphia incorporated ''Famous'' into its name the day it opened in 1923. Now in its third generation of management, the Auspitz family is still good-humoredly audacious (David L. Auspitz has ''Chairman of the Board'' printed on his business card) and still producing food to die for. If the deli wasn't famous in 1923, it is now.

What superlative might be appropriate for you to add to your association's name? _____

BUILDING A PERSONALITY
INTO A NAME (continued)

Names that Advertise for You

Some organizations have names that:

- Describe the product or service

- Are catchy, clever, and memorable, and

- Appeal to the consumer's sense of humor.

If the names use rhyme or alliteration, so much the better. Here are some examples.

▶ *Unravel Travel* describes what a travel agent can do for a hapless traveler lost in a sea of confusing fare wars and incomprehensible restrictions.

▶ *Rent-A-Wreck* provides rental cars for people willing to settle for less luxury and lower rates.

▶ *Hue and Cry Alarm Systems* illustrates the function of an alarm system in a picturesque manner.

▶ *A Positive Sign* makes signs, banners, etc.

▶ *A Clean, Well-Lighted Place for Books* says everything that needs to be said about this bookstore.

▶ *The Guiltless Gourmet* distributes salsa that contains no fat, sugar or oil, in health food stores.

▶ *Let the Good Chimes Toll* is a company that makes wind chimes.

FINDING THE RIGHT NAME FOR YOUR ENTITY

Many businesses are named after the owner. Is this wise or merely an indulgence of ego?

- If the owner is well-known in the community or an expert in the field, using the name will give the establishment credibility.

- If the owner is a celebrity, using the name will give the establishment instant recognition.

- If the owner is not well known, consider adding something else to the name to give it a more specific definition—for example, Jones Travel might expand its name to Jones' Deluxe Travel without losing its identity or position in the Yellow Pages.

Even an establishment that is stuck with a name, such as a government office, can use some imagination by adding extra dimensions to it. The province of Alberta, famous for its Canadian Rockies scenery, has added image to its name. Alberta Tourism uses ''Alberta, in all her majesty'' on brochures and maps. And the logotype for Alberta is designed so that the first letter resembles a mountain peak.

LET'S GET PERSONAL— WHAT ABOUT YOUR ESTABLISHMENT'S NAME?

Do you like the name of your organization?

_____

Did you choose the name or did someone else name it?

_____

Does it define the essence of your enterprise?

_____

Have customers ever been confused by the name and what it conveys?

_____

Is the name easy to understand when pronounced over the phone, or do callers ask that it be repeated?

_____

Will this name be appropriate for your organization in five years?

_____

Would you consider changing or modifying the name?

_____

If there were no risks, hassles, expenses or complications involved in changing your association's name, what would you call it?

_____

SECTION

IV

How to Become an Image Analyst

THE IMAGE DETECTIVE

You might find it helpful to compare several businesses of the same type—the way we did with travel agencies. At this stage you can be more objective if your own sense of competitiveness isn't involved, so try starting with a field other than your own. Select a category that has easy access, and several competitive locations near you.

Here are some possibilities. Select one from the list or choose one of your own.

- Real estate agencies

- Barber or beauty shops

- Drug stores

- Restaurants

- Clothing stores

- Furniture stores

- Movie theaters

- Others _____

_____

_____

IMAGE DETECTIVE CHECKLIST

THE IMAGE DETECTIVE'S CHECKLIST

Outside Impressions

Drive past the establishment, then walk past the front of the building.

	Yes	No
Is the enterprise easy to spot from your car with an easy-to-read sign?	☐	☐
Does the sign convey the nature of the business and its specialty?	☐	☐
Are the business hours posted?	☐	☐
Is the neighborhood busy and prosperous? Are all storefronts occupied? Is the block neat and well-maintained?	☐	☐
Are people on the streets well dressed?	☐	☐
Is parking easy to find?	☐	☐
Is parking free?	☐	☐
If the enterprise has its own parking lot, is it full of customer's cars?	☐	☐
Are the cars new and expensive?	☐	☐
Are the vehicles 4×4s and pickups?	☐	☐
Is the location accessible by public transit?	☐	☐
Does the enterprise seem appropriate to its location (does its image "fit" the neighborhood)?	☐	☐
Can you see into the store or office from the street?	☐	☐
Is there a window display?	☐	☐
Are price tags part of the display?	☐	☐
Is the display fresh and organized?	☐	☐
From what you've seen so far, is this a successful operation?	☐	☐
If you were a prospective customer, would you enter?	☐	☐

Inside Impressions

Now go in.

	Yes	No
Is the door open?	☐	☐
Is there a smell that you notice? Is it pleasant?	☐	☐
Is the atmosphere quiet?	☐	☐
Is there background music? Is it appealing?	☐	☐
Is the room you've entered neat and clean?	☐	☐
Do you have to hunt around for someone to assist you?	☐	☐
Is the staff polite and competent?	☐	☐
Is their dress appropriate?	☐	☐
Within a few seconds of entering, do you feel interested and comfortable?	☐	☐
If you were a customer, would you stay?	☐	☐

If you answered ''no'' to most of the questions on the checklist, think about how the business could improve its image. Does it need to relocate? Is it a question of redecorating? Does the product or service need to be upgraded?

If you answered ''yes'' to most of the questions, you have probably just researched a successful business in action.

IDENTITY CRISIS LESSON

When energetic Françoise, a retired restaurant owner, moved to a small town in New Zealand, she soon grew restless.

''Buy a restaurant,'' her new neighbors advised her.

So Françoise opened her own restaurant. ''I decided to give these small-town people a chance to experience fine continental cuisine,'' she said. ''I put on lace tablecloths and classical music. But nobody felt comfortable.

''So I lightened up the music and made the decor more casual.

''Instead of wearing a black dress and high heels when I greeted my customers, I started dressing more like them.

''I thought I was going to show them something; instead, they showed me. I couldn't run the restaurant just the way I wanted to. I had to learn what they expected, what they wanted. Then my new restaurant caught on.''

Another Identity Crisis: Kimberley, British Columbia

Not too long ago, residents of the mining town of Kimberley, British Columbia, didn't like to admit they lived there, according to Clark Brentwood's article in *Beautiful British Columbia Magazine's* winter 1991 issue.

Since mines don't produce forever, buildings in Kimberley hadn't been built to last. By the early 1970s, storefronts were looking drab and neglected, and business was far from prosperous.

But when the town got a new mayor, Jim Ogilvie, it also got an idea for a brand-new image. The community decided to give itself a facelift with a Bavarian theme. The downtown *Platz* (plaza) was equipped with a huge cuckoo clock. Merchants adorned store and restaurant fronts with the exposed timber patterns typical of Bavaria. Homeowners started fixing up their houses.

Recently, the inevitable announcement was made that the lead and zinc mining operation (employing 700 workers) will shut down by the year 2000. Yet rather than pulling out and leaving deserted mine shafts and exposed tailings, the mining company is spending millions to landscape their property and has agreed to let part of it be used for a museum.

One unexpected result of the mountain community's new image is that cottage industries are moving in. German craftsmen, hearing about Kimberley's similarity in climate and appearance to a Bavarian village, have come to town along with their businesses. A goldsmith, glassblower, restauranteur and cabinetmaker are already in residence. The cabinetmaker brought his house, too—shipping in and reassembling a traditional German building that had been in his family for generations.

Without its unusual image, which caused merchants and homeowners alike to take pride in the community, Kimberley might be on the way to becoming just another deserted mining town.

HOW YOUR ORGANIZATION FITS INTO YOUR COMMUNITY

While you've been sleuthing local business establishments, you've also been getting a feel for what kind of image your entire community projects. And that's important to understand in terms of how your enterprise will (or does) fit in.

	Yes	No
Are there one or more shopping centers in town?	☐	☐
Is the main street downtown a popular shopping destination?	☐	☐
Are there lots of big department stores?	☐	☐
Are there discount or factory outlet stores?	☐	☐
Are small, personalized service shops popular?	☐	☐
Do expensive boutiques do well?	☐	☐

What type of shopper or client is targeted by businesses in your community? Check those that apply.

_____ Young professionals   _____ Female shoppers

_____ Retired folks   _____ Male shoppers

_____ People on a tight budget   _____ Other

_____ Big spenders

_____ Teenagers

_____ Ethnic groups

WHO ARE YOUR PROSPECTS?

Try to visualize how your establishment fits into the community image. If the main street of your city is full of factory outlets, how will the expensive antique china shop you hope to open fit in?

If you're operating a big discount camera shop surrounded by designer boutiques, how will your ideal customer find you?

If you've noticed that most of the businesses in town cater to the retirement-age set, this won't be the place to open your skateboard shop.

It's best if your enterprise is located near other businesses that will appeal to the same type of customer. That's why discount and factory outlet stores tend to locate near each other in the same shopping centers.

SECTION

V

Your Competition's Image

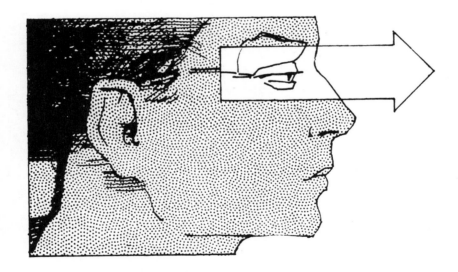

TAKING A LOOK AT THE COMPETITION

You've learned to be an image detective. Now that you're an expert, you're ready to scout your competition on their home turf.

Look at the competition's image in two ways. First, pretend that you're a customer for the product or service they're offering. Second, think like an entrepreneur. How can you make your organization's image better than theirs? Use the image detective's checklist on the next page to scope out your competition.

IMAGE DETECTIVE'S CHECKLIST— SLEUTHING THE COMPETITION

Outside Impressions of a Competitor

Drive past the establishment, then walk past the front of the building.

Is the enterprise easy to spot from your car? _____

Is the neighborhood busy and prosperous, or are there deserted storefronts nearby?

_____

Is the neighborhood neat or run-down? _____

Are people on the streets well dressed? _____

Is parking easy to find? _____

Is parking free? _____

If the enterprise has its own parking lot, is it full of customers' cars—or empty?

_____

Are the cars new and expensive? 4x4s or pickups? _____

Is the location accessible by public transit? _____

Is the outside of the building clean and well maintained? _____

Is there an easy-to-read sign in front? _____

Does the establishment's sign clearly indicate the nature of the business and its specialty?

_____

Are the hours the business is open posted? _____

Does the enterprise seem to fit into the neighborhood? _____

If this is an office building, is there a business directory inside that is easy to read?

_____

Is the door open? _____

Can you see into the store or office from the street? _____

Is there a window display? _____

Are price tags part of the display? _____

Is the display fresh and organized, or tired, dusty, and faded? _____

What is your first impression? _____

_____

_____

_____

_____

_____

_____

Does this look like a successful operation? _____

If you were a prospective customer, would you enter or leave now?

_____

IMAGE DETECTIVE'S CHECKLIST
(continued)

Entry-Level Impressions

Now walk inside.

Is there a smell that you notice? Is it pleasant? _____

Is the atmosphere quiet or noisy? _____

Is there background music? Is it appealing and appropriate? _____

Is the room you've entered neat and clean? Dusty or cluttered? _____

If the receptionist or sales clerks are occupied, do they acknowledge your presence with a glance or a smile, or ignore you?

_____

Does the customer have to hunt around for someone to assist? _____

What kind of attitude does the staff portray (polite, indifferent, rushed, bored, etc.)?

_____

Do the staff members use good grammar? _____

Do they seem knowledgeable? _____

Is the mode of dress of the employees appropriate? _____

How do you feel within the first few seconds of entering (interested, comfortable, uneasy, annoyed)?

_____

Is there a spacious look, or are quarters cramped and crowded? _____

Now, looking at your own entity through the eyes of an objective image detective, apply these same questions to your establishment.

WHERE YOUR ENTERPRISE FITS INTO THE COMPETITIVE PICTURE

When you're studying the competition, keep in mind how your unique and special enterprise will fit in. Make sure you don't overlap or copy the image of an established entity.

If your competition is located in a shopping mall, they're probably paying high rent for high visibility and easy access to walk-in customers. But they may have to spend less on advertising; when they do advertise, it may be a part of a shopping-center cooperative ad where expenses are shared among several businesses.

Where is the rest of the competition? Do they maintain an upstairs office in a neighborhood away from the main street? They may have an existing clientele that knows where to find them. Perhaps they do most of their business by mail and telephone. Or maybe they're short on cash and are saving rent by locating upstairs. How can you tell?

If the rest of the buildings on the block look prosperous, the establishment is probably doing well with a good following. If the neighborhood looks poor and run-down, however, the competition is probably down on their luck.

Now you know where your competition is. Where should your enterprise be positioned?

BE DIFFERENT FROM COMPETITORS

YOUR ENTITY'S IMAGE WILL DIFFER FROM YOUR COMPETITION'S

Now that you have examined your competitors' businesses, think about how you can make yours different.

Does your competitor specialize in one line, or handle a choice of products?

_____

Is this clearly evident in the competitor's image? _____

How does your business duplicate the activities of this competitor? _____

_____

Is your image like the competitor's in that area, or can you make yours different or better?

_____

How is your entity different from this competitor? _____

_____

How does your own image indicate this difference? _____

_____

Can you think of a unique way to present your enterprise's image? _____

_____

Can you think of a way to make your store or office look different from those of your competitors? _____

_____

Can you think of something you could add to or change about the name of your enterprise to make it more clearly defined, or more catchy, than that of your competitors? _____

_____

_____

_____

THE LESSON OF TWO COMPETING INSURANCE COMPANIES

Fred was recently rear-ended in an accident which damaged his car's bumper, and he suffered a minor whiplash injury. Fortunately, both he and the driver who hit him were insured.

Fred called his carrier, Insurance Company A, for instructions. "Go to our claims office to file a report. Or you can try to get reimbursement directly from the other driver's insurance company," they said. "But that might be a hassle."

First, Fred visited his local Buick dealer to get an estimate of repairs from the body shop. It came to just under $2,000.

Insurance Company A's poorly-groomed receptionist, when he arrived, snapped, "You can't come here without an appointment—didn't your agent tell you that?" Fred explained that he'd just called and been told to come in. "Well, maybe one of the adjusters can see you," said the receptionist grudgingly. "Sit over there and wait." The reception area featured a video showing staged accidents with dummies, which left Fred feeling even more shaky.

Finally, he was ushered into an office. "We estimate your damage at only $750," the adjustor said, glancing at his paperwork dubiously. "Since your policy has a $500 deductible, here's a check for $250. We'll apply to the other driver's carrier for the other $500—but that can take up to a year." Her tone of voice implied, "You're getting more than you deserve, Buster!"

"What about the doctor bills?" Fred ventured. "For the whiplash?"

"Medical bills for any actual injuries will be taken care of—eventually," the adjustor said.

Then Fred went across the street to the other driver's carrier, Insurance Company B, where he was received politely without an appointment. He was greeted by a well-dressed, friendly claims adjuster who wrote a check for the full amount remaining on the automobile repair estimate. "We'll pay for a rental car while yours is in the shop," offered the adjuster. "And just have your doctor send bills for treatment and any therapy you need to your insurance company; they can forward them over to us for payment."

THE LESSON OF COMPETING INSURANCE COMPANIES (continued)

When it was time to renew his automobile insurance, Fred changed his account from Company A to Company B.

Don't forget: advertising, company reputation, decor and all other aspects of an image can be destroyed by the demeanor of an organization's staff.

S E C T I O N

VI

How Image Can Target and Screen Prospects

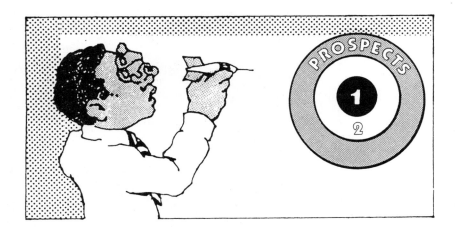

YOUR IMAGE AS A SCREENING DEVICE

One of the important functions of your image is to act as a screening device that will save both you and your prospects a lot of time by appealing to one segment of the marketplace and discouraging inappropriate business.

This may sound negative, but it's simply realistic: Most establishments will appeal to some prospects and turn others off.

Can your establishment be all things to all people? _____

_____

Do you have a supermarket approach to marketing and advertising? _____

_____

Or do you have a special target market in mind? _____

_____

There is an increasing trend in the business community to find a particular niche in the marketplace and to promote that niche. If you have a special area of expertise, consider promoting it.

HOW TO SCREEN CUSTOMERS WITHOUT SAYING A WORD

1. A San Francisco travel agency has a name that screens and defines its customers. It's called Dirt Cheap Travel, Inc.

If you wanted to book a luxury cruise, would you call Dirt Cheap Travel? If you wanted the lowest airfare to London or South America, would you call Dirt Cheap Travel?

2. Imagine that you're shopping for records, CDs or tapes of your favorite type of music. You enter a shop that has a conservative decor, mature salespeople, soft carpets and a well-modulated stereo system playing Mozart. Will this store be likely to carry your favorite country and western selections?

You approach another shop that is pulsating to the rhythm of rap music so loud that customers must shout at the young clerks to be heard. Standup cardboard displays of garishly dressed rock stars decorate the supermarket-styled store. Will the salesclerk with the punk hairdo be able to find your favorite classical CDs?

Both of these stores screen their customers. You know before you enter whether each one has what you need.

SECTION

VII

Crafting and Fine-Tuning Your Entity's Image

LOGOS, MASCOTS AND SLOGANS

Logos, mascots and slogans can help an organization keep on target with its image.

Qantas Airlines has built a consistent and recognizable image with its mascot, the grumpy yet appealing koala bear. The freight railroad, Union Pacific, has a slogan that builds confidence both inside and outside the organization:

WE CAN HANDLE IT!

When American Business Communications needed a new logo, owner Dee Tozer considered about 40 versions before settling on one.

Old Logo    New Logo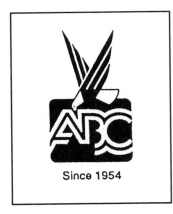

The new logo cost about $2,000. ''Rather than having the designer do layouts for our invoices, business cards, cartons and packages, we simply bought the logo and are using it in various in-house designs for our other needs. If we'd had the same designer do layouts for everything, it would have cost about $20,000,'' said Tozer.

Does your organization need a logo, mascot or slogan? Does it have one? Does your logo need to be modernized? Before making a final decision on a logo, particularly one using colored ink, make sure it holds up under black-and-white reproductions such as photocopying and faxing.

HOW YOUR GOALS CAN KEEP YOU ON TRACK

Before you can achieve success, you must know what your goals are. Now is the time to think about them.

What is the goal or mission statement of your organization?

_____

_____

_____

_____

_____

_____

Is your organization's name consistent with that goal? Why?

_____

_____

Is the store or office front consistent with that goal?

_____

_____

Is your location consistent with that goal?

_____

_____

Is the decor of the interior of the store or office consistent with that goal?

_____

_____

Are the logo and lettering used on signs, stationery and business cards consistent with each other and that goal?

_____

_____

Are the personalities and skills of the staff consistent with that goal? Why?

_____

_____

Are the goals of the organization consistent with your personality?

_____

_____

Have the goals of the organization changed over time? Has the image kept up, or does it need updating?

_____

_____

Does the staff's mode of dress enhance or detract from that goal?

_____

_____

In what other ways does your organization's image fit—or not fit—with its goals?

_____

_____

Taken as a whole, does your organization's image hang together harmoniously and consistently?

_____

_____

HOW CLOTHES MAKE OR BREAK AN IMAGE

People today have more opportunity to dress the way they choose at work. Freedom of expression and comfort are now important considerations.

It no longer seems essential, in many occupations, to adopt a dress code that is someone else's formula for professional success. Yet not all taboos have been lifted. Consider your reaction if you were a customer, client or patient in these scenarios.

► You walk into an elegant and expensive rooftop restaurant. The decor is wood paneling and polished brass, a string quartet is playing and the menu includes fine wines. You're ready for a festive meal to celebrate a special occasion, but your enthusiasm wanes when your waiter greets you in paint-spattered overalls worn through at the knees.

► You have been feeling nervous and stressed lately, so you decide to consult a psychologist. As she shakes hands and introduces herself, you're a little surprised to see that she is wearing a skin-tight leather jump suit with a chain belt.

Inappropriate clothes can be distracting. They can leave the client or patient feeling uncomfortable and confused. And they can cause you to question the competence—or even the sanity—of the person you're trying to do business with.

Uniforms

A uniform can save time and eliminate misunderstandings if your enterprise needs instant identity.

A stranger wearing shorts, a tank top and sandals rushes into your office. He thrusts a clipboard at you. "Sign here," he commands. What would you do? Insist on seeing his ID? Order him to leave immediately? Call the police?

Now replay the above scenario, but dress the man in the familiar brown shirt and pants uniform that identifies him as a United Parcel Service courier. You'll cooperate quickly, without qualms or questions.

A uniform is also a handy way to separate customers from employees in a crowded store and to provide a readily identifiable source of assistance.

Uniforms can identify authority figures such as police officers, clergy, firefighters, airline pilots, train conductors and customs officials. And uniforms can denote members of a staff who have a particular function, such as chefs, doctors and nurses.

Would uniforms or a dress code enhance or detract from the image of your enterprise?

_____

If you had only yourself to consider, what would you like to wear to work?

_____

What do you think your ideal customer expects you to wear? _____

_____

What would your staff prefer to wear? _____

What do you think your ideal customer expects your staff to wear? _____

_____

Are there any issues about style of dress that you should discuss with your staff?

_____

What kind of clothing best expresses the image you would like your enterprise to portray?

_____

HOW ONE OF THE FIVE BEST BANKS IN AMERICA BROKE THE "DRESS FOR SUCCESS" STEREOTYPE

Maverick banker Carl J. Schmitt, CEO of University National Bank and Trust Company in Palo Alto, California, has cracked the staid, pretentious image of "a typical banker" wide open. Basing his organization's image on his goal of understated elegance, Schmitt's bank is unusual.

"We have a dress code here for the men: You must wear a long sleeved shirt (no short sleeves), but you can't wear a jacket. When we hire people from other banks, they have a hard time with that at first, because it changes the image they have of themselves—and, of course, that's the point," Schmitt says.

In November 1991, *Fortune* Magazine rated University National Bank and Trust Company among the "five best banks" in the United States. *Fortune* described the bank's unique image, saying it "creates a clublike aura of desirability."

YOUR INVISIBLE IMAGE IS IMPORTANT, TOO

The telephone has completely changed the way we relate to other people. The images you project in a personal encounter, such as dress, grooming, how neat your desk looks, whether you are plain or good-looking, thin or fat—none of these elements enter into your telephone personality. What a caller hears becomes all important, because it is the only source of information. And callers size us up within seconds of our picking up the telephone.

Every enterprise has an "invisible image" that makes an impression on prospects. The first words used to greet a telephone caller, the background music (or lack of it), the noise level of equipment or machines in the building—even the number of times the caller hears the word "no"—are all part of an organization's invisible image.

If your organization gets lots of telephone inquiries, your invisible image may be even more important than your visible one.

What kind of experiences have you had when making calls to other businesses? How often has your first impression of an organization been tarnished because you were:

- Put on hold for more than 30 seconds

- Cut off

- Been answered by a "click" followed by a long hold

- Answered by a hostile or indifferent person

- Offended by someone who was making remarks to somebody at their end of the line instead of listening to you

- Told "We're closed" by a janitor or someone who refused to take a message

Make sure that whoever answers your phones is skilled in telephone techniques, understands the goals of the organization and has a pleasant personality. Remember that your entity's telephone personality is its invisible image—and is vitally important to your success.

YOUR IDEAL CUSTOMER OR CLIENT

Unless you are the only business or service around that offers the product or service you do, you'll need to select the segment of the market you want to appeal to. Visualize your ideal customer. This won't necessarily be the average customer you have now.

My ideal customer is:

_____ Male

_____ Female

_____ Single

_____ Married

_____ Divorced

_____ Widowed

_____ Teenage

_____ Child

_____ Senior citizen

_____ Homeowner

_____ Involved in a particular sport

_____ Owner of a particular product

_____ Physically fit

_____ Handicapped

_____ Other

My ideal customer has the following characteristics:

_____ Age

_____ Educational level

_____ Income bracket

_____ Occupation

_____ Other

Here are some things about my establishment's existing image that my ideal customer will find attractive:

_____

_____

_____

Here are some things about my establishment's present image that my ideal customer might not like:

_____

_____

_____

Here are some things I can change about my establishment's image to make it more appealing to my ideal customer:

_____

_____

_____

Here are things I can change to make it more convenient for my ideal customer:

_____

_____

_____

DREAMING UP AN IDEAL IMAGE

You may decide that you are satisfied with your organization's image just as it is. Or you may find that it needs updating, a change of direction or a complete overhaul.

Forgetting, for now, about the constraints of location, budget and size, let your imagination soar. Brainstorm as if anything were possible.

What kind of an ideal visible image would you choose?

_____

_____

Would you change the goals for your organization? How?

_____

_____

Your ideal logo and typestyle would be:

_____

_____

If you could locate your organization anywhere that you liked, would you move it to another country or another city? Where would that be?

_____

_____

Does your ideal organization have a theme that sets it apart from the competition?

_____

_____

Describe an appropriate mascot for your dream organization.

_____

_____

What would an ideal slogan be?

_____

_____

The decor for your ideal office would be:

_____

_____

The ideal employees for your organization would be:

_____

_____

What else would your ideal image consist of?

_____

_____

_____

_____

_____

_____

_____

_____

MODIFY YOUR IDEAL IMAGE TO MEET REALISTIC EXPECTATIONS

Go back over your brainstorming list for your ideal image. Let's see how you can upgrade your existing image.

What would be easy to change?

_____

_____

_____

_____

What would be possible to change?

_____

_____

_____

_____

What would be affordable to change?

_____

_____

_____

_____

What would you like to change that seems difficult or impossible now?

_____

_____

_____

_____

UPDATING AN EXISTING IMAGE

Even brands that have become household words—such as Campbell's Soup—need to have their images updated occasionally.

Classic identities like Campbell's are usually altered subtly so that the familiar image is maintained without jarring the customer who has grown up with the product.

The little girl with the umbrella who has graced the Morton's Salt box for decades has had her clothes and her figure changed many times to keep up with current styles.*

1914   1921   1933   1941   1956   1968

*Morton's Umbrella Girl Design and ''WHEN IT RAINS IT POURS'' are registered trademarks of Morton International, Inc. and are used by permission of Morton International, Inc.

UPDATING AN EXISTING IMAGE (continued)

Does your organization need to update its typestyle, signs, decor, logo or packaging?

_____

How can you do this without losing your association's identity?

_____

Will you need professional help to accomplish this?

_____

> "Unless there is some fundamental change in the ways a company does business, the basic tools of image and identity—the logo and other communications items—generally last about twenty years. All too often, they are not reviewed until the end of that cycle, which is almost always too late for easy repair."—Clive Chajet, _Image by Design_ © 1991, by Clive Chajet. Reprinted with permission of Addison-Wesley Publishing Company.

Changing an Image to Meet New Consumer Expectations

The recessionary economy of the 1990s, along with an increasing concern for the environment, has changed the marketing plans of many businesses. For example, a Wisconsin shoe manufacturer has changed its advertising strategy, according to Judith Block's article in the September 1991 issue of _Entrepreneur Magazine_.

"Promoting luxurious lifestyles is out. My new ad will stress . . . quality, comfort and natural materials."

"There won't be Rolls Royces with my shoes, or pearls draped over them," said John Stollenwerk, president of Allen-Edmonds Shoe Corporation.

The management of Hyatt Hotels is becoming more sensitive to environmental issues. According to the October 1991 issue of *Hospitality World*, Patrick Cowell, regional VP of Hyatt Resorts Hawaii, claims that responsible resorts offer ''the perfect environment for preservation and educational efforts, providing large areas of land and water, irrigation, and landscapers.'' Two of Hyatt's Hawaii resorts now employ ''wildlife directors,'' who have received government rehabilitation permits to provide help for species in need. Hyatt Regency Kauai has developed a protected environment for some of Kauai's endangered plants and an educational program about them.

Have your clients expressed new concerns or values?

_____

_____

_____

_____

Has your enterprise considered incorporating these concerns into its image?

_____

_____

_____

_____

How can your organization's image adapt to such a change in values?

_____

_____

_____

_____

WHEN TO CALL THE IMAGE DOCTOR

We've been talking about ways to recognize, clarify and express your entity's image. Managing your company's image yourself may be feasible, particularly if you're just starting an enterprise. With some skill and a bit of luck, your image should be working as a good ambassador for your organization.

On the other hand, if your image is not doing the right kind of job for your organization, you should be well aware of that fact by now.

Not everyone has the time, patience, or talent for do-it-yourself image building and updating. If you have recently:

- Taken over ownership or management from someone else

- Changed your location, goals or product line

- Altered your way of doing business because of new technology

- Been subject to growth, downsizing or mergers

- Realized that the gold shag carpets you liked so much in the 1970s are out of date and that if you replace them the 1970 furniture will have to go, too

- Noticed that your envelopes, business cards and brochures have three typestyles, all of which look dated

You may decide to call for professional help. Perhaps you'll hire the services of an interior decorator or a graphic artist. Or you may need an image doctor to do a complete overhaul.

If you know deep down that your image needs to be completely restructured and coordinated, where do you start?

Known variously as ''corporate identity specialists,'' ''image management consultants,'' ''marketing and design firms,'' ''strategic-design consultants,'' and ''identity management and design consultants,'' these professional image doctors can offer help—and they make house calls!

Such companies can send specialists to analyze your enterprise from within the corporate structure. They can also observe it from the outside to judge how you are communicating with the public.

Now that you understand the dynamics of image-crafting and have analyzed your own image, you're in a better position to profit from the help of a consultant. You won't run the risk of having an outsider, who doesn't know your organization nearly as well as you do, design a new image that doesn't fit the unique personality of your entity.

There are several excellent design and identity consulting firms. A few include Ford & Earl Associates, Inc., Schecter Group, Pentagram, Lippincott & Margulies, Aspach, Grossman & Portugal and Landor Associates.

Landor Associates is a firm with offices throughout the world. Their clients include Mercedes Benz, Westin Hotels, Levi Strauss, Sony and SAS. But not all Landor's clients are giants of the Fortune 500 variety. They accepted an assignment to design an ice cream container for a small California company. A packaging job of this type might run about $30,000.

For a total corporate identity program designed by a company like Landor or Lippincott & Margulies, you would expect a price tag of $80,000–$300,000.

Exactly what do the identity program designers do? Clive Chajet, chairman and CEO of Lippincott and Margulies, says that a corporate identity consultant could ''develop image objectives; establish coordinated communications strategies; alter the company's signage, its logo, its corporate communications, and/or its name; refurbish campaigns to change the image of a division or perhaps only the image of the CEO; set up an investor relations department within the company to communicate with Wall Street; develop an advertising campaign; modify communications architecture so that over time it will shape a new image for the company as a whole.''* That's quite an effort.

---

*Clive Chajet, *Image by Design* © 1991 by Clive Chajet. Reprinted with permission of Addison-Wesley Publishing Company.

WHO USES AN IMAGE DOCTOR, AND WHEN?

According to Jerry H. Kline, a vice president of Ford & Earl Associates, Inc., of Troy, Michigan, "Most people call the image doctor when something significant is happening to the organization—like a change of location."

His company has handled corporate identity programs for a:

- Steel mill
- Cement company
- Restaurant
- Department store
- Utility company
- Golf equipment shop
- Hospital
- Physician
- Beauty salon

The beauty shop, which was having a decorator redo its interior, needed a new logo and updated graphics for its business cards, appointment cards, stationery and a bag that customers used to carry home hair-care products.

Kline, the owner of the beauty shop, and her public relations expert first conferred for an hour about what the beauty shop wanted. Then Kline went to work. Questions he typically addresses are whether:

- The firm is conservative, modern, experimental
- The firm sells products or services
- The firm is a high-tech or low-tech business
- The company will stay in its present line of business or expand into new areas*

A week later, Kline came back to the beauty shop with three logo and typestyle choices. When the beauty shop owner made her selection, Kline took the job to a printer and made sure that the business cards, appointment cards, stationery and the carry-home bag were done to Ford & Earl's specifications.

For just under $2,500 and in only three weeks, the job was finished. Projects for large organizations can take more than a year, according to Kline, and are much more expensive.

---

*Jerry H. Kline, *Office Systems*, November 1991.

NON-PROFITS HAVE IDENTITIES, TOO

Earth share is a non-profit organization that coordinates workplace fund-raising campaigns on behalf of its 27 affiliated organizations, such as the World Wildlife Fund and the Nature Conservancy. Earth Share approached Landor Associates to develop a new corporate identity to help achieve the organization's goals: to get people involved in the notion that we are all "investors or shareholders" in the earth.

Earthshare wanted their new logo to be emotional (humanity interacting with the Earth) with overtones of sophisticated professionalism (to appeal to corporate decision-makers). Landor Associates created an Earth Share identity that protrays a human figure reaching for the stars, suggesting that we all must share in the solutions of environmental problems. It also suggests human empowerment and a call to action.

Earth Share℠

SUMMARY: HOW TO LAUNCH YOUR IMPROVED IMAGE CAMPAIGN

Now that you're more aware of images and how they work, you can look at your own organization's image through new eyes.

Keeping your image congruent, timely and appropriate is a continuous project. It's not something you can fix once and forget. But this dynamic process can be a creative, enjoyable and rewarding one.

What is the most important thing you've learned about images?

_____

_____

_____

Has your opinion of your entity's image changed?

_____

Will you take steps to improve that image?

_____

How will the improvements you plan to make enhance your:

- Staff's sense of mission and morale?

_____

- Customer relations?

_____

- Profits?

_____

- Position among your competitors?

_____

LET'S GET STARTED

The first step I'll take to enhance my organization's image will be:

_____

_____

_____

_____

_____

_____

_____

_____

Once I've done that, I'll:

_____

_____

_____

_____

_____

_____

_____

_____

My timetable for getting started is: _____

I'll have these goals completed by: _____

BIBLIOGRAPHY

Chajet, C. *Image by Design: From Corporate Vision to Business Reality.* Addison-Wesley Publishing Company, 1991.

Dible, D. *Up Your OWN Organization!* Simon & Schuster, 1985.

Ewen, S. *All Consuming Images.* Harper Collins Publisher (Basic Books), 1988.

Gee, B. *Winning the Image Game.* Page Mill Press, 1991.

Haskett, M. *Design Your Own Logo.* Self-Counsel Press Inc., 1991.

Hawken, P. *Growing a Business.* Simon & Schuster, 1988.

Laing, J. *Do-It-Yourself Graphic Design.* Facts on File, 1984.

Levinson, J. *Guerrilla Marketing Attack.* Houghton Mifflin, 1989.

Louis, H. *How to Handle Your Own Public Relations.* Nelson Hall, 1976.

Lyons, J. *Guts: Advertising from the Inside Out.* Amacom, 1987.

Phillips, M. *Honest Business.* Random House, 1981.

Ries, A., & J. Trout. *Positioning: the Battle for Your Mind.* McGraw-Hill, 1980.

Settle, R. & P. Alreck. *Why They Buy: American Consumers Inside and Out.* John Wiley & Son, 1986.

Swann, A. *How to Understand and Use Design and Layout.* Writer's Digest Books, 1987.

NOTES

FOR OTHER FIFTY-MINUTE SELF-STUDY BOOKS
SEE THE BACK OF THIS BOOK.

NOTES

FOR OTHER FIFTY-MINUTE SELF-STUDY BOOKS
SEE THE BACK OF THIS BOOK.

NOTES

FOR OTHER FIFTY-MINUTE SELF-STUDY BOOKS
SEE THE BACK OF THIS BOOK.

NOTES

FOR OTHER FIFTY-MINUTE SELF-STUDY BOOKS
SEE THE BACK OF THIS BOOK.

NOTES

FOR OTHER FIFTY-MINUTE SELF-STUDY BOOKS
SEE THE BACK OF THIS BOOK.

$$\boxed{\textbf{NOTES}}$$

FOR OTHER FIFTY-MINUTE SELF-STUDY BOOKS
SEE THE BACK OF THIS BOOK.

ABOUT THE FIFTY-MINUTE SERIES

We hope you enjoyed this book and found it valuable. If so, we have good news for you. This title is part of the best selling *FIFTY-MINUTE Series* of books. All *Series* books are similar in size and format, and identical in price. Several are supported with training videos. These are identified by the symbol ⓥ next to the title.

Since the first *FIFTY-MINUTE* book appeared in 1986, millions of copies have been sold worldwide. Each book was developed with the reader in mind. The result is a concise, high quality module written in a positive, readable self-study format.

FIFTY-MINUTE Books and Videos are available from your distributor. A free current catalog is available on request from Crisp Publications, Inc., 95 First Street, Los Altos, CA 94022.

Following is a complete list of *FIFTY-MINUTE Series* Books and Videos organized by general subject area.

Management Training (continued):

Personal Improvement:

Human Resources & Wellness:

Human Resources & Wellness (continued):

Communications & Creativity:

Customer Service/Sales Training:

Small Business & Financial Planning:

Adult Literacy & Learning:

Career/Retirement & Life Planning: